Vegan Spanish Cooking

Andy Luttrell

Dedicated to Shalini, who has had her share of gazpacho, some better than others.

Acknowledgements

Thanks to everyone I met in Spain who shared their knowledge of Spanish food with me: Ana, David, Maria, Blanca, Borja, Miguel Ángel, Darío, Javi, and especially, Pablo and Bea.

I also owe a debt of gratitude to the scores of Spanish blogs and YouTube videos I consulted in trying to figure out how to recreate authentic Spanish recipes. My Spanish language skills got a workout as I watched about twelve YouTube videos of Spanish cooks in their own kitchens describing how they make *cocido*.

If you speak or read Spanish, there are also a number of good vegan blogs and websites in Spain. You can learn more at:

CreatiVegan (http://www.creativegan.net/)
La Dimensión Vegana (http://www.dimensionvegana.com/)
Gastronomía Vegana (http://www.gastronomiavegana.org/)
Spanish Sabores (http://www.spanishsabores.com/)

Granada

Recipes

Extra Information

Although I want this cookbook to contain a bunch of great recipes, what I really want is to share an appreciation for Spanish food and culture in general. So, each recipe opens with some background, but also, throughout the book, I've included a bunch of extra information about topics related to Spanish food and culture. Here are those extra bits:

Introduction

T hank you so much for supporting this project of mine. I've spent the last several years on an inspiring and challenging task: interpreting Spanish food and culture for a vegan lifestyle.

In 2013, I had the opportunity to spend six weeks living in Madrid. I'm a graduate student, and one of my research collaborators is from Madrid. Although he works at a university in Spain, he spends some time each year in the United States. I had gotten to know him well, and of course I jumped at the chance to take a trip to Spain to work with his students in Madrid. The next year, I lucked out yet again and got to make another visit.

Although there's no clear reason for it, I had always wanted to visit Spain. Learning Spanish was always something I enjoyed, and even though I stopped taking classes after high school, I continued to practice and learn the language independently. Over time, I got it into my head that someday I'd visit Spain.

I must say, right off the bat, that Spain is lovely. Its culture is vibrant, warm, and welcoming. Its history is deep, and its cities, diverse. I spent most of my time in Madrid, which is a city I've come to love, but I've also traveled to other Spanish cities, including Barcelona, Granada, Toledo, and more.

My visits to Spain also put me in touch with plenty of locals who showed me around, and gave me a genuine Spanish experience. Through these friendships, I have learned many insider insights on Spanish food and culture, these insights having been shared in many bars, restaurants, and homes where people are cooking and eating authentic Spanish food.

There's a caveat to this glowing praise, however. Spanish food glorifies meat. The national indulgence is its famed *jamón ibérico*, which is a special type of ham that Spaniards take a lot of pride in. Seafood is also heavily represented, given that most of the country is surrounded by water. So what's a vegan to do?

Well, fortunately, Spanish food does celebrate vegetables in many delicious ways. *Gazpacho*, for example is about as Spanish as it gets, and it's totally vegan. Even still, sticking to a strict vegan diet would seem to deny one the full pleasure of Spanish cooking.

Although I did encounter a number of great vegetarian restaurants with fully vegan menus, I must admit that I ate egg and dairy in Spain. I realize that this dietary exception (reminiscent of Peter Singer's "Paris Exception") may not strike all readers of this book as acceptable, but it was a choice I made to balance my personal food values with the value I place on experiencing other cultures.

Me in Segovia at the top of the Alcázar, 2013

Once I returned home, however, I set out to recreate the many wonderful things in Spanish cuisine that I was able to eat while I was there. Not only that, I wanted to veganize the foods that I was only able to see others eat. This effort has amounted to this collection of fully vegan recipes that I hope captures the spirit of Spanish food and culture without using animal products of any kind.

I've had the pleasure of bringing many of these recipes to potlucks and hosting Spanish themed parties myself, and these are hits for vegetarians and meat-eaters alike. I've also had some of my Spanish friends come through the U.S., and I've gotten them to try my attempts at their country's cuisine. I'm happy to report that they were impressed.

So thank you again for purchasing this cookbook. It has been an amazing project, and I hope you find a special place for Spanish cooking in your home as well.

The Spanish flag flying in a Barcelona plaza

Soups and Stews

I could have made a book with just Spanish soups because I love them that much. So I hope you like soup because there are plenty of recipes in this book to satisfy any of your soup needs!

In this section, there are soups and stews of every variety. There are chilled soups like the classic *gazpacho*, but other less familiar ones like *salmorejo* and *ajoblanco*. There are hearty stews like my beloved Spanish lentil stew, and there are creamy delights like the creamy garbanzo soup.

Get ready to enjoy the delights of Spanish soup!

Gazpacho
Chilled Tomato Soup

If there's one Spanish food that you're familiar with, it's probably *gazpacho*. Once summer hits, the temperature is at its peak, and fresh tomatoes flood the farmers' markets, there's little else I want beyond a cold *gazpacho*.

Until I went to Spain, though, I didn't think I liked *gazpacho*. That's because in the U.S., every exposure I had to "*gazpacho*" was a chunky mix of tomatoes and other vegetables that reminded me of cold, watery salsa. Although I'm told that there's such a thing as chunky *gazpacho* in Spain, I never saw it. Almost everywhere I went in Spain, there was a creamy, luscious *gazpacho* that doesn't come close to the chunky mess I had seen before. This was the real stuff, blended into a smooth soup and served as the perfect appetizer to a lunch on an outdoor *terraza* or as a quick midday snack.

Over the summer, whenever I get back from the farmer's market, I can quickly blend up a big batch of *gazpacho* and put it in the fridge to cool. That way, I've got fresh, cold *gazpacho* ready for me over the next several days.

At this point, I generally put my *gazpacho* together by taste and eyeballing what looks right to me, so there's natural variation from one batch to the next. Below, however, is a good base recipe that comes from my observations and memories from Madrid. Feel free to make it more tomato-heavy, increase the vinegar or oil, or whatever makes you happy. You'll hit upon the perfect arrangement for your taste, and it'll be hard not to make a ton of it.

It's common to garnish *gazpacho* with little chunks of the vegetables that go inside: chopped tomatoes, cucumber, and bell pepper. It gives a nice crunch to what's otherwise a silky smooth soup.

Serves 4

Ingredients

1 ½ - 2 lbs tomatoes (about 4 medium/large tomatoes)
½ lb cucumber, peeled and seeded (about 1 medium cucumber)
1/3 lb green bell pepper, cored and seeded (about 1 small bell pepper)
2-4 cloves garlic, peeled
1 ½ teaspoons salt
1 ½ tablespoons white wine vinegar
¼ - ½ cup good Spanish olive oil
About 4 inches of a stale baguette (optional)

For a garnish later, finely dice some of the tomato, cucumber and bell pepper. Having about ¼ cup each of diced vegetable will be plenty.

For a thicker, creamier *gazpacho*, take the crust off a hunk of stale bread and soak for 10 minutes or so in water. Squeeze some of the water out and add the soggy bread to the blender bowl.

Put all of the ingredients (except what you kept for garnish) in a blender, including the soaked bread (if using), and blend to a smooth puree. (For a smoother *gazpacho*, you can push it through a strainer, too) Taste and add salt, vinegar, or oil as needed. Move the *gazpacho* to the refrigerator and let cool for at least an hour.

To serve, pour out the *gazpacho* into shallow bowls (I often serve this up in white coffee mugs). Top with the diced vegetables, and drizzle a tiny bit of olive oil over the top if you'd like.

Farmer's Market Tip

The great thing about *gazpacho* is that you can use ugly tomatoes, and nobody's the wiser after everything gets blended together. Try seeing if there's anyone at your market selling less-than-perfect tomatoes at a discount. Sometimes they're labelled "scratch and dent," "seconds," or "salsa tomatoes." If you don't see a sign, you can also just ask the people at the stand—sometimes they have a box under the table of tomatoes that didn't look good enough to put out. Just trim any bruises or unappetizing blemishes off and toss the rest in the blender. Now you can afford to make twice as much *gazpacho*!

Melon Gazpacho

Gazpacho de Melón

Watermelon *gazpacho* is pretty common, but a stroke of genius following a farmers market visit resulted in this cantaloupe version, which makes for a refreshing summer treat.

Serves 4

Ingredients

1 ½ - 2 lbs orange tomatoes (about 4 medium/large tomatoes)
1 lb cantaloupe or watermelon, seeded and cut into 1-inch chunks)
1/3 lb green bell pepper, cored and seeded (about 1 small bell pepper)
1 clove garlic, peeled
1 ½ teaspoons salt
1 ½ tablespoons white wine vinegar
¼ - ½ cup good Spanish olive oil
About 4 inches of a stale baguette (optional)

Soak bread in water for at least 10 minutes, if using. Squeeze some of the water out and add the soggy bread to the blender bowl.

Blend all ingredients very well in a blender. Chill for at least an hour in the refrigerator before serving.

Strawberry Gazpacho

Gazpacho de Fresas

Serves 4

Ingredients

1 ½ - 2 lbs tomatoes (about 4 medium/large tomatoes)
1 lb strawberries, stemmed (about a dozen medium/large
    strawberries)
1/3 lb green bell pepper, cored and seeded (about 1 small bell
    pepper)
1 clove garlic, peeled
1 ½ teaspoons salt
1 ½ tablespoons white wine vinegar
¼ - ½ cup good Spanish olive oil
About 4 inches of a stale baguette (optional)

Soak the bread in water for at least 10 minutes, if using. Squeeze some of the water out and add the soggy bread to the blender bowl.

Blend all ingredients very well in a blender. Chill for at least an hour in the refrigerator before serving.

Although the strawberry seeds get ground pretty well in the blender, for a completely smooth *gazpacho*, push the blended mix through a strainer before refrigerating.

Olive Oil

Aceite de Oliva

You may be surprised to learn that Spain routinely produces roughly 3 times the amount of olive oil as Italy. In the U.S., anyway, people seem to have associated "olive oil" with Italy only. In fact, about a third of Spain's olive oil exports are to Italy, where it gets bottled and sold though Italian brands that command higher prices. You may be familiar with the *Bertolli* brand of Italian olive oil. According to an article in *The Economist* in 2014, some of the oil sold under that brand is actually Spanish olive oil. Change is on the horizon, though. In 2014, the U.S. imported more Spanish than Italian olive oil for the first time ever.

Is there a difference? I have been assured by many Spaniards that Spanish olive oil is much better than other olive oils, and I've come to believe it. Spanish olive oil is indeed very good, which you might expect given how much olive oil is in Spanish food! For both cooking and using raw (e.g., *gazpacho*), the quality of the oil makes a big difference.

Much of Spain's olive oil production comes from Andalucia in Southern Spain, but other major olive-producing regions include Castilla – La Mancha and Extremadura. In these regions, the climate is just right for cultivating olives that become great olive oil. The Mediterranean climate throughout Spain provides a fertile environment for olives to thrive, and if you take a train to get from one Spanish city to another, you're bound to whiz past patch after patch of old olive trees.

So for a true Spanish experience, look for extra-virgin Spanish olive oil at your local supermarket.

Green Gazpacho

Gazpacho Verde

It's the same *gazpacho* rules but with one remarkable difference: no tomatoes allowed.

My first sampling of a *gazpacho verde* was in a vegetarian restaurant in Madrid. At first I thought it was just *gazpacho* made with green tomatoes, but the waitress was quick to correct me. *Gazpacho verde* is a celebration of green produce (and sure, sometimes that includes green tomatoes), and it's made in the same familiar style of a classic *gazpacho*.

Of course, some will tell you that it's no stand-in for regular *gazpacho*. When I mentioned to my friend in Madrid that I had *gazpacho verde* at lunch that day, his brother chimed in to say, "that's not *gazpacho!*" Nevertheless, it's a healthy and delicious starter to a summertime lunch.

When I set out to make *gazpacho verde* at home, I was amazed to find that the number of ways to make it seems to equal the number of people who've tried. This recipe is my particular favorite, but I've seen recipes that include any and all green fruits and vegetables: spinach, avocado, celery, fennel, zucchini—you name it. So keep an eye out for anything green at the grocery store, and it's bound to work in *gazpacho* form.

Serves 4

Ingredients

1 cucumber, peeled and seeded
1 green pepper, cored and seeded
1 Granny Smith apple, cored
2 – 3 green onions

Flat-leaf parsley (about half a handful torn off of a bunch)
2 cloves garlic, peeled
½ serrano pepper, stemmed and seeded (optional)
¼ cup good Spanish olive oil
1 tablespoon white wine vinegar
1 teaspoon salt
¼ cup water

For a garnish later, finely dice some of the cucumber, green pepper, apple, and green onions and set aside.

Chop up the cucumber, green pepper, green apple (leave the skin on), and green onions (remove the white bulbs) into chunks and put into a blender.

Add the rest of the ingredients to the blender and blend until smooth. Add more water as needed to get everything to blend and to reach your desired consistency. Let it chill in the refrigerator for an hour or so, and you're ready to serve.

Additional Notes

As with regular *gazpacho*, you can also push the soup through a strainer to achieve a smoother final soup. I'm happy with the semi-coarse texture because that's where the fiber-y good stuff is, and the beauty of a *gazpacho verde* is its healthfulness.

You can also consider adding a half cup of plain vegan yogurt for a creamier *gazpacho*.

Salmorejo

Although *gazpacho* is the undisputed king of cold Spanish soups, *salmorejo* (sahl-more-AY-ho) is just as good at providing a refreshing cool down on a hot Spanish day. Of course I had heard of *gazpacho*, but the first time I tried *salmorejo*, it became an instant favorite. It's a thick, cold tomato soup that's also naturally vegan.

My friend Pablo first introduced me to *salmorejo* and showed me how he makes it. I've included his added flair in the recipe below (adding just a little bit of green pepper for "freshness") although it's not traditional in making this soup. The hallmark of *salmorejo* is the use of stale bread, soaked in water to bring its softness back. The bread, when combined with a healthy portion of olive oil, makes for a thick, rich soup that's perfect in the summer when tomatoes abound.

In Spain, it is common to garnish *salmorejo* (and in particular, *salmorejo cordobés*) with diced boiled egg and bits of serrano ham. Although I like this soup all on its own, consider topping this with bits of a vegan bacon to recreate the meaty complement to the rich tomato flavor.

Serves 4 - 6

Ingredients

1 lb tomatoes
1 clove of garlic
¼ medium green bell pepper (optional)
6 inch piece of a baguette (about 150 grams); stale bread
     works well in this
1 teaspoon of salt
1 ½ tablespoons white wine vinegar
½ cup good Spanish olive oil

If your bread has a tough crust, just scoop out the inner white bread from the baguette. Traditionally, the bread is soaked in water until it is soft. Soaking it for the amount of time it takes to prepare the other ingredients is usually enough. If I'm using bread that's already pretty soft, though, I sometimes forgo the soaking altogether. Squeeze out the excess water from the bread and add to the blender bowl.

Add the tomatoes (no need to peel or seed, but I get rid of the top part where it used to hang onto the stem), garlic, salt, and vinegar to the bread in the blender. Blend until everything is smooth, 3-5 minutes. At this point, give the *salmorejo* a taste and adjust the vinegar and salt as you like. This is also your chance to adjust the thickness. If you find that it's too thick for you, add some water, but if it could be thicker, add a little bread. After making your adjustments, blend everything again.

Finally, set the blender to low and slowly stream in the olive oil. Once it's done, chill in the refrigerator for at least an hour.

Variations

One Spanish vegan blog (**danzadefogones**) proposed a great idea for serving *salmorejo*: on toast with avocado. Toast a slice of bread, spread some *salmorejo* over it, and top with a few slices of avocado for an indulgent breakfast or appetizer. Crack some black pepper on top if you'd like, too.

Cucumber Salmorejo

Salmorejo de Pepino

The same cool, smooth, and delicious experience you get with a classic tomato-based *salmorejo* can also be adapted to other refreshing vegetables. This recipe is essentially the same as a normal *salmorejo* but with cucumber in place of the tomatoes. The result is a refreshing, cool soup that serves as a great summer first course or even a good quick drink that doubles as a snack!

Serves 2 - 3

Ingredients

2 large cucumbers, peeled
2 inches of a stale baguette
2 tablespoons olive oil
1 ½ tablespoon vinegar
1 clove of garlic, peeled (optional)
½ teaspoon salt

If your bread is pretty stale, soak it in water for 10 minutes or so. Squeeze some of the water out and add the soggy bread to the blender bowl.

Blend everything until smooth in the blender. Chill for at least an hour and serve cold.

Almond Garlic Soup

Ajoblanco

Another in the family of chilled soups, this is sometimes called *"white gazpacho."* Its thickness comes from bread and ground almonds, and it all comes together with the unmistakable pungency of raw garlic. Top with sliced green grapes for a refreshing summer soup.

Serves 2 - 3

Ingredients

2 inches of a stale baguette
1 cup almonds, soaked and peeled (or about ¾ cup pre-purchased blanched slivered almonds)
1 – 1 ½ cup water
1 tablespoon vinegar
2 tablespoons olive oil
2 cloves of garlic, peeled
½ cup green seedless grapes, sliced, *for garnish*

First, soak the stale bread in water for 10 minutes or so until it's soft. Remove the bread from its soaking liquid and add it to a blender bowl. You can also use an equivalent amount of fresh baguette for this, in which case you can skip the soaking step. Add the rest of the ingredients (except the grapes) and blend until very smooth.

Chill in the refrigerator for at least an hour and serve cold, garnished with sliced grapes and an extra drizzle of olive oil.

Peeling Almonds

If you are working from raw almonds, bring two cups of water to a boil and remove from heat. Soak whole almonds in the just-boiled water for 3 – 4 minutes. Drain the almonds and allow to cool. At this point, their skins should slide right off.

El Parque de Buen Retiro, Madrid

Spanish Stewed Lentils

Lentejas Guisadas

L entil soup seems to be the stock and trade of any vegan home cook, and this one is my absolute favorite. Every time I make this, I'm surprised at just how much warm, wonderful flavor gets packed into this homey stew.

This is adapted from a recipe in the classic Spanish cookbook, *1080 Recetas de Cocina* ("1080 Recipes"). I'm told that this is the Spanish equivalent of the Betty Crocker cookbook. Every family has a copy, and it's a common gift for young people when they move out of their family's house. I've left most of the original recipe intact except to modify and clarify a few steps and ingredients.

Although this recipe was naturally vegan in its original printed form, when I showed the photo of it to my Spanish friend, the first thing she said was, "It's missing *chorizo*." Well, I don't think it's missing anything, and it's as deeply rich and comforting as any meat-heavy stew.

Serves 6

Ingredients

1 lb green/brown lentils
1 onion
2 cloves garlic, peeled and minced
6 cups water (feel free to substitute up to 4 cups with vegeta-

ble broth)

4 tablespoons olive oil

3 inches of a baguette (stale bread even better), sliced into 4
pieces

½ teaspoon smoked paprika (*pimentón dulce*)

14.5 oz can of diced tomatoes or 1 large tomato, peeled, seeded, and chopped

2-3 tablespoons chopped parsley

1 teaspoon salt

Peel the onion and cut it in half. Dice one half of the onion, and put it aside for later. With the other half, cut it in half and put the two onion quarters right into your soup pot. Peel one clove of garlic, smash it, and put the whole smashed clove in the soup pot as well. Rinse the lentils, removing any little stones if you see them, and put the dry lentils in the pot. Cover with 6 cups of liquid, bring to a boil, cover and reduce to a simmer for about 30 – 40 minutes or until lentils are tender.

When the lentils have cooked, keep the lentils warm on a low heat. In a separate pan, heat the olive oil and lightly fry the bread slices, flipping once to ensure a nice brown crispiness on each side of the bread. Move the fried bread to a paper towel-covered plate.

Add the diced onions to the oil you used to fry the bread, and sauté until golden brown. When the onion becomes fragrant, add the garlic and sauté for another few minutes. Add the smoked paprika for 30 seconds to let its flavor bloom. Add the tomatoes and let the whole mix cook and reduce for about 10 minutes.

With a mortar and pestle (or a coffee grinder), grind the fried bread pieces into crumbs. You can also chop the bread to bits on a cutting board.

Add the onion and tomato mix, the breadcrumbs, and parsley to the cooked pot of lentils. Stir, raise the heat to get everything up to the right temperature, season with salt, and add more liquid if the lentils have absorbed quite a lot.

Serve warm. Garnish with any remaining chopped parsley.

Galician Stew

Caldo Gallego

The term *caldo* means "broth," so it's important that you use a tasty broth in this soup. Typically, the broth in recipes like this is flavored from the meat that's cooked at the beginning of the recipe, but of course, we'll have to take another route. Using our seitan *chorizo* helps, but you'll still want to start with an already delicious broth.

Caldo Gallego traditionally includes: greens (often cabbage or turnip greens), potatoes, white beans, and pork (either *chorizo*, ham, or bacon). Here I've gone with kale and seitan *chorizo* (although you could leave the *chorizo* out entirely). The whole thing makes for a simple, comforting stew when the weather gets cold.

Serves 4

Ingredients

1 – 2 tablespoons olive oil
1 large onion, peeled and diced
2 cloves of garlic, peeled and sliced
6 cups vegetable broth
1 Russet potato, peeled and diced (about 1-inch cubes)
3 carrots, peeled and cut into 2 – 3-inch long pieces
½ bunch kale, stemmed and chopped
1 15-oz can of white beans (Navy, Great Northern, Cannelini, etc.)
1 vegan *chorizo* sausage (page 56), cut into about 10 slices (optional)

Heat the olive oil in a soup pot. Add the *chorizo* slices and cook until browned on both sides. Remove and let rest on a paper towel-covered plate.

Add the onion and garlic to the hot oil and cook 5 – 8 minutes, until aromatic. Mix in the potatoes and carrots and cover with broth. Raise the heat until the liquid is boiling, cover, and reduce the heat to let simmer for 10 – 15 minutes while the potato cooks all the way through.

When the carrots and potato are cooked, add the white beans and kale. Let cook another 5 minutes until the kale has wilted. Finally, add in the *chorizo* (if using) and let everything heat through on the stove for another 5 – 10 minutes.

Spinach and Garbanzo Stew

Potaje de Garbanzos y Espinicas

I f your only association with garbanzo beans or chickpeas is canned beans, get ready to change that. Both this recipe and *cocido* (page 95) are great examples of how *garbanzos*, cooked slowly with flavorful liquid, are surprisingly delicious all on their own.

My favorite thing about this is that the starch from the bean leaches out into the cooking liquid over time, thickening it as it goes. This contributes all the more to the deep, comforting texture and flavor that makes this the perfect cold weather dinner.

Potaje is a popular Spanish meal during Lent and dates back to medieval times. Oftentimes during Lent, it is made with codfish (*bacalao*), and it seems common to include hard-boiled eggs when serving *potaje*. Of course, this recipe does away with both elements, but with a dish as rich and warm as this, it doesn't feel like anything is missing.

Note that starting from dry beans means that this isn't a quick preparation. It isn't much work, but be sure to get the beans on the stove about 2 hours before you'd ideally like to eat.

Serves 6 - 8

Ingredients

1 lb dry garbanzo beans (soaked; see note)

1 onion, peeled and diced

2 – 3 carrots, peeled and chopped in 1-inch circles

3 cups vegan chicken-flavored broth (or any vegetable stock)

3 cups water

2 teaspoons salt (adjust depending on saltiness of broth)

3 tablespoons olive oil

2 cloves garlic, chopped

1 teaspoon smoked paprika (*pimentón dulce*), optional

14 oz can diced tomatoes (or two fresh tomatoes, diced)

10 oz chopped spinach

To prepare, soak the dry garbanzos overnight in plenty of water plus a tablespoon of salt. The salt serves to brine the beans and will keep them in tact throughout cooking.

On cooking day, drain the beans from their soaking liquid and move to a stock pot (the one I use is 6 quarts). Add the carrots, half of the chopped onion, broth, water, and 2 teaspoons of salt. Bring to a boil and reduce to a simmer; leave the beans to cook for an hour, partially covered.

After an hour, add 2 tablespoons of the olive oil and simmer on low until the beans are tender (about another half hour). At this point, scoop out and reserve 2 cups of the cooking liquid. You'll be able to add this back in if you need more liquid, but more importantly, you can use this to add liquid without losing flavor if you reheat this and eat the leftovers on another day.

During the last half hour of cooking the beans, in a large frying pan, heat the remaining tablespoon of olive oil and sauté the remaining onion and garlic until translucent (5 – 6 minutes). If you're using the smoked paprika, add it now and let it bloom in the oil for 30 – 60 seconds. Add the canned tomatoes and let cook until the liquid in the tomatoes reduces (5 – 10 minutes).

Once the beans are tender to your liking, add the onion and tomato mixture along with the chopped spinach to the stock pot and give everything a good stir. Give everything a chance to cook through to the point that the spinach is thoroughly wilted (5 minutes or so). Take a taste and add salt as necessary and add back some liquid if you find it's too thick.

White Bean Stew

Fabada

T he Spanish name for this is technically *Fabada Vegana* (or "vegan *Fabada*"), which is maybe the most fun thing to say. Fun names aside, this is a hearty bean stew from the Spanish region of Asturias. Technically, the hallmark of this dish is the type of beans traditionally used: *fabes*. They're large white beans that cook up with a creamy interior. If you can get your hands on these and want the authentic experience, go for it. I've opted for the easier-to-obtain large lima beans (or butter beans), usually available at everyday grocery stores. If you still have trouble and happen to have some navy beans or cannellini beans stored in the cupboard, you can use those too.

Serves 6

Ingredients

1 lb dried large lima beans, soaked overnight
2 – 3 tablespoons olive oil
1 loaf vegan Ham (recipe on page 59), cubed (optional)
1 *Chorizo* sausage (recipe on page 56), sliced (optional)
1 onion, peeled and diced
2 cloves of garlic, peeled and chopped
1 – 1 ½ teaspoons smoked paprika (*pimentón dulce*)
1 tomato, diced
Pinch of saffron
3 carrots, peeled and chopped
6 cups water
Salt, to taste

Heat the oil in a large soup pot. Brown the vegan ham and/or *chorizo*, if you're using it, and place on a paper towel-lined plate for later. Next add the onions and garlic to the remaining olive oil, cooking until translucent (roughly 5 minutes). Add the smoked paprika, letting its flavors bloom in the oil for 15 seconds or so. Now add the tomato, beans (drained of their soaking liquid), carrots, and water. Crush the saffron between your fingers and add it to everything else.

Bring to a boil, lower the heat, and let simmer for an hour, until the beans are cooked through and creamy (but still intact). Add the vegan ham and/or *chorizo* back to the stew if you're using it, and let everything heat through. Salt to taste.

Somewhere in Barcelona...

Cream of Zucchini Soup

Crema de Calabacín

Serves 2 - 3

Ingredients

1 tablespoon olive oil
1 small onion, peeled and chopped
2 zucchinis, chopped
1/8 teaspoon ground nutmeg
1 teaspoon salt
1 large potato, peeled
2 cups water (or less if you want a thicker soup)
Croutons for serving (optional)

Heat olive oil in a large saucepan, sauté onions until translucent (about 4 minutes). Add zucchini and sauté for another 4 – 5 minutes. Mix in ground nutmeg and salt, and add the potato pieces.

Cover with water, bring to a boil, and reduce to simmer for 15 – 20 minutes or until the zucchini and potato pieces are soft.

Move to a blender and blend very well. Serve hot, topped with croutons if you like.

Creamy Garbanzo Soup
Crema Castellana de Garbanzos

The first taste of this soup is a warm reminder of *cocido madrileño* (page 95) without the same amount of work. You might even be able to make it right now with what you have in your pantry and refrigerator. It's disarmingly simple, but I really, really love this soup.

This simple soup, a typical meatless dish that appears in Spain during Lent, serves as a great first course on cold autumn or winter days. It's also a great opportunity to use up leftover garbanzo beans (like after making a big batch of *cocido madrileño*).

Serves 4

Ingredients

1 teaspoon olive oil
1 large onion, peeled and chopped
4 cloves of garlic, peeled
2 – 3 Roma tomatoes, diced
1 ½ teaspoons smoked paprika (*pimentón dulce*)
¼ - ½ teaspoon ground nutmeg
2 14.5 oz cans of garbanzo beans (or the equivalent of cooked garbanzos), reserve a few beans for garnish
2 – 3 large carrots, peeled and chopped in large pieces
4 cups vegetable broth
1 teaspoon salt (depending on saltiness of broth)

Heat the olive in a saucepan and sweat the onions and garlic cloves (3 – 5 minutes). Add the tomatoes, paprika, and nutmeg and stir, cooking for another 3 minutes until the tomatoes reduce and thicken. Finally, add the beans, carrots, and broth. Raise the heat and bring to a boil, and then lower the heat, and simmer, covered, for 20 minutes.

Once the vegetables are cooked through, blend the soup into a smooth puree. I like to use an immersion blender for this, but you can instead opt for a standing blender. Salt to taste, and you're ready to serve!

Serve hot topped with a couple whole garbanzo beans and croutons if you have them.

Sauces

Like any great cuisine, Spanish food involves a handful of delicious sauces. From simple *alioli* to the bold, striking *bravas* sauce to the exotic *mojo picon*, the Spanish know their sauces. All of these sauces have countless applications. Any of them would be perfectly at home zipping up grilled or steamed vegetables, but they're also used in particular applications that I cover elsewhere in this book.

Let's get saucy...

Garlic Mayonnaise

Alioli

You will find this all over Spain. Plop it on your paella or dip any cooked vegetable in it. *Alioli* is beloved, but it's really just adding garlic to mayonnaise, which you can do if you make your own mayo or even if you buy pre-made mayo.

If you make your own mayonnaise, just blend a few cloves of garlic with the non-dairy milk before adding any of the oil.

If you already have mayonnaise, simply crush 3 cloves of garlic with some kosher salt and mix into a cup of mayo. Classically, people crush garlic using a mortar and pestle, but you could instead opt for a small food processor or even just crush the garlic with a chef's knife and go to town on it with the back of a fork. For a little more acid, mix in 1 – 2 teaspoons of lemon juice.

Bravas Sauce

T here are so many ways to make the sauce for that Spanish classic, *patatas bravas*. Some recipes call for a lot of mayo and some don't use it at all. Some people use fresh tomatoes, some use ketchup, and some nix the tomatoes altogether. The common denominator is the spice—two spices, that is: *pimentón dulce* and *pimentón picante*. These are the sweet and hot varieties of Spanish smoked paprika (see page 47).

In Spanish, *"bravas"* means "bold," so the sauce always comes with a kick, and it's up to you how much of a kick you're willing to take. This recipe uses ground cayenne because *pimentón picante* is hard to find.

Use this as the topping in a classic *patatas bravas* (page 64), but you'll find plenty of things to put this on. You can pour it over your *tortilla de patatas* (page 65) like they do at "Las Bravas" in Madrid or try it over steamed or grilled asparagus as a tasty side. Once you taste this sauce, you shouldn't have a hard time thinking of things to put it on.

Makes 1.5 cups

Ingredients

1 tablespoon olive oil
½ yellow onion, peeled and chopped
3 cloves garlic, chopped
3 teaspoons smoked paprika (*pimentón dulce*)
½ - 1 teaspoon ground cayenne pepper
1 tablespoon flour
15 oz canned diced tomatoes, or equal weight in fresh diced
    tomatoes (no need to peel)
1 teaspoon salt
1 teaspoon sugar
3 tablespoons vegan mayonnaise (optional)

Heat the olive oil in a medium saucepan. Add the onion and garlic and sauté until golden (about 4 - 5 minutes). Don't let them brown.

Add the smoked paprika and cayenne and mix into the onion and garlic. Do this for just 15 seconds or so to aromatize the spices without burning them. Sprinkle the flour into the mix and stir to incorporate. This simple roux will help develop a thicker sauce.

Add the canned tomatoes and bring to a simmer. If you're using fresh tomatoes, you may want to add a few tablespoons of water to prevent the tomatoes from sticking and burning. Let cook for about 5 - 10 minutes—just enough time for the tomatoes to cook down into a chunky sauce.

Add the salt, sugar, and vegan mayonnaise (if using) and blend everything into a smooth puree in a blender or with a handheld blender stick.

Smoked Paprika

Pimentón

S moked paprika (or *pimentón*, in Spanish) has become a popular spice, it seems. Although it has recently caught on in the U.S., it has been a mainstay of Spanish cuisine for many years. The peppers that ultimately made up this spice came from the Americas—Christopher Columbus brought them back when he returned to Spain in the 15th century. Years later, people began smoking and drying these peppers and grinding them into the spice at the center of so many Spanish dishes.

There is one part of Spain that is revered for its pimentón: **la Vera** in Extremadura (just southwest of Madrid). In fact, just as wines in Spain are noted by their Denominación de Origen (D.O.), a national system intended to regulate quality of geographic locations of origin, *pimentón* has its own D.O. in la Vera. As such, people refer to the best quality smoked paprika as *pimentón de la Vera*.

Smoked paprika begins as small red peppers, and they are then smoke-dried with smoke from slow burning oak wood.

The dried peppers are finely ground using large stone wheels that very slowly grind the dried peppers so as not to produce too much heat in the process (which can result in off-flavors and color).

Although in the U.S., it's common to find "smoked paprika," in Spain there are actually three types of *pimentón*. The one that gets labeled as "smoked paprika" in the States is *pimentón dulce* (or "sweet paprika"). There is also, however, *pimentón picante* (or "spicy paprika"), and *pimentón agridulce* (or "medium paprika"). All have their place, of course, but it's the sweet variety that is most common, and lucky for us, it's the easiest to find in the U.S.

Be wary of cheap imitations, however. I was excited to find smoked paprika at a local grocery store at a very low price, but when I got it home and opened the package, I realized that all they had done was add smoke flavor to regular sweet paprika. In a pinch, this will add the color and slight smoky experience, but it really is no match for the good stuff.

I'm always amazed at how much this one little spice can add to food. It's a great spice to have around when cooking for non-vegans as well. The smoky depth it adds to stews like *fabada* and to side dishes like *patatas revolconas* provide a distinctly meaty taste without any of the animal involvement.

Many of the recipes in this book rely on this spice, so it's a good one to have if you want to try your hand at Spanish cooking. I hope, though, that as you see its utility in these traditional Spanish recipes, you'll also develop an affinity for it in other preparations as well.

Romesco Sauce

I had been making *romesco* sauce before going to Spain, but I was surprised that I didn't see it on too many menus. While I was in Segovia, however, at the restaurant in the Parador hotel, which overlooks the beautiful city, I had artichokes with this famed Spanish sauce. As with most "traditional" recipes, there are plenty of different ways to make it. That said, this recipe represents my favorite take on it, highlighting delicious roasted red peppers, toasted almonds, and just enough olive oil to bring it all together.

Makes 2 cups

Ingredients

1 lb tomatoes (about 2 medium-large tomatoes)
1 red bell pepper
4 cloves of garlic, unpeeled
3 inches of stale baguette
½ cup almonds, peeled
2 tablespoons vinegar
1 tablespoon smoked paprika (*pimentón dulce*)
1 teaspoon salt
¼ cup olive oil

Pre-heat the oven to 425°F. Rub the tomatoes, the red bell pepper, and the garlic cloves with a little bit of olive oil, just to coat it. Place the tomatoes, bell pepper, garlic cloves, and the bread on a baking sheet and slide into the hot oven. After 20 minutes, remove the garlic and bread and keep on a plate. Turn the tomatoes and the pepper and let them roast for another 20 minutes.

While the other ingredients are roasting in the oven, toast the almonds in a dry skillet. Be careful not to burn the nuts, but heat them to the point that they begin to brown and smell toasty.

Add everything but the oil in the blender or food processor. Blend until it reaches a smooth puree. Keep it blending and slowly pour in the olive oil until everything is incorporated.

Using Romesco Sauce

Typically this sauce is served on meats and fish. Certainly that won't do for us. This sauce is delicious over roasted fingerling potatoes, but it is especially good on a grilled vegetable sandwich. On a grill or cast iron skillet, grill long slices of zucchini, portabella mushroom, and/or eggplant. Fill a toasted sandwich roll with the grilled vegetables and sliced tomatoes and spread *romesco* sauce (generously) on the upper piece of bread.

Mojo Picon

Both *mojo picon* and *mojo verde* come from the Canary Islands. They are delicous, slightly acidic, and a little spicy. They go great on all sorts of vegetables; I even enjoy the simple pleasure of dipping bread in them. One traditional use for *mojos* is in *papas arrugadas* (page 80), a unique dish in the Canary Islands. Whether you use these for that or for something else, enjoy the delight that a good *mojo* brings.

Makes 1 cup

Ingredients

3 – 4 cloves of garlic, peeled
1 red bell pepper, stemmed and seeded
1.5 teaspoons ground cayenne
1 tablespoon smoked paprika (*pimentón dulce*)
1.5 teaspoons ground cumin
3 teaspoons white wine vinegar (or apple cider vinegar)
1/3 cup good olive oil
1 teaspoon salt

First, process the garlic and red pepper into a paste in a blender jar or food processor. Then add the cayenne, smoked paprika, cumin, vinegar, oil, and salt and process into a chunky sauce.

Mojo Verde

Makes 2 cups

Ingredients

6 cloves of garlic
1 bunch of cilantro
1 green bell pepper, stemmed, seeded, and chopped.
3 tablespoons white wine vinegar (or apple cider vinegar)
½ - ¾ cups good olive oil
½ - 1 tespoon salt

Although it's fine to leave the stems on the cilantro, I cut off the bottom bit of the bunch that doesn't have many leaves. Puree everything until smooth in a blender or food processor.

Spanish Faux Meats

I tend to agree that one shouldn't need faux meats to survive on a vegan diet. Of course seitan isn't a necessary food group. Of course packaged faux meat products are loaded with preservatives. But sometimes it's just fun to get a little closer to the authentic experience without sacrificing your values. So for this reason, I've included a few vegan versions of popular Spanish meat products.

Meat is at the center of so much Spanish cuisine. Paging through a Spanish cookbook, nearly every recipe contains *jamón* or *chorizo*. It's just the way things are done. So here are some vegan versions in case you desire to add an extra Spanish protein kick to your tapas party. I stopped eating meat years before traveling to Spain, so I can't really say how good these are as imitations of their authentic counterparts. They are tasty, though. When I whip up a quick *morcilla* tapa, I eat plenty more than I expect to.

Most of my personal involvement with Spanish food has been in Madrid, however, and I know that along the beautiful coasts of Spain, seafood reigns supreme. Shrimp, or *gambas*, are an integral part of the cuisine. That said, I haven't had tremendous luck crafting my own vegan seafood alternatives, but I invite you to give it a try! Let me know what you come up with.

Morcilla Sausage

I t's amazing how much I like these vegan sausages given how much the authentic version makes me squirm. In Spain, *morcilla* is a blood sausage, and it's surprisingly popular. Were it not for my desire to make a vegan version of *cocido madrileño* (page 95), I would never have thought to try to make a vegan version of this.

I haven't ever tasted the real thing, so I cannot vouch for the authenticity of this *morcilla*, but what I can say is that it's really tasty. Real *morcilla* is dark black, and there are visible bits of rice when the sausage is cut into pieces.

To keep the black color, this recipe uses black beans and dark soy sauce (but you can also use regular soy sauce). The rice is still there, and so are the cooked onions, which is what sets this apart from other vegan sausages you might have tried.

Give these a try—you'll be surprised. Dark, delicious vegan sausages that are miles away from the original version based on pig's blood. I'd choose these ones any day.

Makes about six 6-inch sausages

Ingredients

1 teaspoon olive oil
½ onion, finely diced
2 cloves garlic, minced
¾ cups cooked short-grain white rice (I use sushi rice)
15 oz can of black beans, drained and rinsed (or equivalent
    volume of home-cooked beans)
1 cup vegetarian broth
2 tablespoons dark soy sauce

1 teaspoon smoked paprika (*pimentón dulce*)
1 teaspoon oregano
1/8 cup bread crumbs
1 cup vital wheat gluten

Before you begin, get your steamer ready so that the water's boiling and you're ready to go when you finish shaping the *morcilla*.

Heat the oil in a small pan and sauté the onion and garlic until they begin to turn brown.

Mash the beans in a large bowl until no whole beans remain. There's no need to make a completely smooth puree, but mash them down to a paste. Add the cooked onion and garlic, cooked rice, soy sauce, smoked paprika, oregano, and bread crumbs to the mashed beans. Fold these ingredients together and use this as your opportunity to give it a taste and any make adjustments (like adding some salt if you need to).

Pour in the broth and mix everything to incorporate the ingredients together. Finally, add the vital wheat gluten. Keep mixing until all of the gluten is incorporated and then continue with your hands, kneading the sausage dough for a few minutes to let the gluten bind.

You'll use this dough to make 6 – 8 *morcilla* sausages. For each sausage, lay down a piece of aluminum foil (roughly a square), and take out enough sausage dough to form a 4 – 6 inch-long sausage. Form the dough into the cylindrical shape, lay it along the edge of the foil closest to you, and roll the dough tightly into the foil, rolling away from yourself. To finish each sausage, twist the ends of the foil tube to keep the dough in its sausage shape.

Put each sausage in the steamer and steam for 30 – 40 minutes. At this point, your *morcilla* are ready, but let them cool for at least 30 minutes before unwrapping and using them in whatever way you intend to.

Serving *Morcilla*

To serve, cut the *morcilla* into slices and lightly fry in olive oil on each side. You can use these to make fried morcilla tapas (page 72) or in *cocido madrileño* (page 95).

Chorizo

Although people in the U.S. have grown familiar with Mexican *chorizo*, the Spanish variety of this spiced sausage is much milder and less familiar to Americans. *Chorizo* can be found in many a Spanish dish, and it owes its signature red color to that Spanish favorite: *pimentón* (smoked paprika).

Whereas Mexican *chorizo* is typically a ground meat product, Spanish *chorizo* is more like salami in that it holds its shape and is eaten with its casing intact. This level of sausage detail, however, is probably not welcome in a book of vegan cooking! Nevertheless, my point is that this distinction is worth paying attention to because some vegan *chorizo* products are made in the Mexican style and aren't easily substitutable in Spanish dishes.

This is adapted from the great vegan *chorizo* sausages in Terry Hope Romero's excellent book, **Viva Vegan**. The biggest change was in the spices, which get it a little closer to Spanish-style *chorizo* (vs. the spicier Latin American versions).

Makes 6 sausages

Ingredients

1 ½ cups vegetable broth or water
14.5 oz can of light red kidney beans
1 ½ tablespoons white wine vinegar
6 tablespoons olive oil
2 cups vital wheat gluten
¼ cup garbanzo (chickpea) flour
3 tablespoons nutritional yeast
2 teaspoons garlic powder
2 tablespoons smoked paprika (*pimentón dule*)

1 teaspoon dried oregano
1 teaspoon ground cumin
½ teaspoon ground clove
½ teaspoon ground cayenne pepper
1 – 1 ½ teaspoon salt

Before you begin, get your steamer ready so that the water's boiling and you're ready to go when you finish shaping the *chorizo*.

In a blender, blend the broth, beans, vinegar, and oil until you have a smooth product. Mix the dry ingredients in a bowl, form a well in the middle and pour in the wet mix from the blender. With a wooden spoon, mix everything to incorporate and then use your hands to knead the dough into a springy gluten-y ball (just a minute or two).

Split the dough into six equal pieces and roll each into a foil tube, using the same technique used to make *morcilla* (page 54). Do this to make all six sausages.

Place the foil-wrapped seitan sausages into a steaming apparatus and steam for about 40 minutes. Cool for another 30 minutes before opening the foil wrappers and witnessing your vegan *chorizo* beauty.

Serving *Chorizo*

Although the steamed seitan *chorizo* sausages are fine on their own, you'll want to lightly fry slices of the sausage in a little olive oil on each side to crisp up the surface. You can serve these fried *chorizo* slices on bits of bread as a tapa or include in whatever recipe calls for Spanish *chorizo*.

Check out the following recipes in this book, which can make use of this *chorizo*: *Caldo Gallego* (page 34), *Fabada* (page 38), *Cocido Madrileño* (page 95), and *Patatas Revolconas* (page 103).

Spanish Pronunciation

Americans have a hard enough time pronouncing *chorizo* when they're talking about the Mexican variety. I'm about to make it a little trickier.

In Spain, they speak Spanish with a peculiar accent. One of the peculiarities is that words that look like they would be pronounced with an s-sound are actually pronounced with a th-sound. That is, when a Spanish word has a *c* or a *z* that you'd normally pronounce like an *s*, you should actually pronounce it with a *th*.

My favorite example is the Spanish word for beer, *cerveza*. To many, this would seem to be pronounced like "ser-VAY-sa." Indeed, that's how it's pronounced in Latin American cultures. In Spain, though, the correct pronunciation is "thare-VAY-tha." Because it sounds like a lisp, I was always terrified that I would be unintentionally mocking people by ordering a "thare-VAY-tha," but I was reassured that I was saying it correctly.

So when it comes to *chorizo*, you might be used to pronouncing it, "chore-EE-so" (as it's pronounced in Latin American cultures), but the way to say it in Spain is, "chore-EE-tho."

Ham

Jamón

When you tell a Spaniard that you are vegan or vegetarian, they love to respond, "But you still eat *jamón*, right?" In Spain, *jamón* is king. Thin slices of *jamón iberico* can be found just about anywhere. They take pride in their unparalleled curing and aging process, so it's no surprise that even the notion that a person would choose not to eat it seems crazy.

Try as I might, though, I doubt I'll ever come up with a vegan alternative that approaches the flavor and texture of true Spanish ham. Of course, I've never actually tasted it, so I wouldn't know if I hit upon that recipe anyway. So for me, there wasn't much use trying to replicate this particular Spanish staple. All the same, however, given its prominence in Spanish cookery, I thought it would be helpful to come up with something that could contribute the cubed smoky protein that serves as the base for so many dishes.

This recipe borrows liberally from the steamed seitan recipes in Terry Hope Romero's excellent book, **Viva Vegan**. The texture of her seitan seemed perfect as the base for cubed vegan "ham." I held onto the basic ingredients and procedure but doctored up the spices to make this a little more on the *jamón* side.

Makes four small "loaves"

Ingredients

1 ½ cups vital wheat gluten
¼ cup garbanzo (chickpea) flour
¼ cup nutritional yeast

1 ½ cups vegetable broth
4 tablespoons tomato paste
2 tablespoons olive oil
2 teaspoons liquid smoke
1 teaspoon ground clove
1 tablespoon smoked paprika (*pimentón dulce*)
1 tablespoon sweet paprika
½ teaspoon black pepper
1 ½ teaspoon smoked salt

Before you get started, set up your steaming apparatus and get the water boiling.

Mix the vital wheat gluten, the garbanzo flour, and the nutritional yeast in a large bowl. Mix all of the other ingredients (broth, tomato paste, oil, liquid smoke, clove, smoked paprika, paprika, black pepper, and salt) in another bowl. Form a well in in the dry ingredients, and pour the wet mix into the well. Mix everything together with a wooden spoon and then knead the dough for a few minutes by hand. Let it rest for 10 minutes and give it another quick knead before portioning the dough into 4 pieces.

Tear out four pieces of foil to wrap each loaf in. Form each piece of dough into a ball, put it in the middle of its piece of foil, and fold the foil around the dough like you're wrapping a present.

Place each wrapped loaf in your steamer, reduce the heat, and steam for 30 minutes. After that time, let the still-wrapped seitan loaves cool on the countertop before moving them to the fridge for at least another hour before using them. This is all in the interest of getting it to the right texture. Once it's been refrigerated, slice it or dice it for you vegan ham needs.

"Meat"balls

Albóndigas

I 'll hold off on talking too much about Spanish meatballs for now. These savory, tasty vegan "meat"balls (lightly adapted from Chef Chloe's "Vegan Meatball Sliders") serve as the base of a popular Spanish tapa. See page 68 for the full package.

Makes a dozen meatballs

Ingredients

2 tablespoons vegetable oil, divided
1 onion, finely chopped
8 ounces sliced mushrooms
2 garlic cloves, minced
1 ½ cups cooked brown rice, cooled
½ cup Italian bread crumbs
¼ cup all-purpose flour
1 tablespoon smoked paprika
2 tablespoons vital wheat gluten
½ cup chopped parsley
1 ½ teaspoons salt

Heat the oil in a wide pan over medium-high heat, and sauté the onions until translucent (4 – 5 minutes). Add the mushrooms and continue cooking until aromatic and the mushrooms have released most of their liquid. Add the garlic and cook for another 2 – 3 minutes.

Transfer mushroom mix to a food processor, and add to it the cooled brown rice, bread crumbs, flour, smoked paprika, vital wheat gluten, parsley, and salt. Pulse until the mixture comes together, but there should still be chunks of rice, mushroom, etc.—no need to fully blend everything.

Transfer everything to a large bowl and knead several times to form the meatball dough, and then break off small pieces, rolling them between your hands, to create 2-inch diameter balls.

Heat the remaining tablespoon of oil in the wide pan over medium-high heat, and fry the meatballs in groups of 4 – 5 until cooked through and browned on the outside.

Tapas

The idea behind tapas is that it's a little bit of food that comes with your drink. In the U.S., tapas restaurants serve up small, shareable bites of Spanish food, so many people think that tapas are just that: small plates you order at a restaurant. In truth, the spirit of a tapa is that it's free!

In Spain (although this varies from place to place), when you order a drink at a bar or small restaurant, you can expect some food to come with it. Sometimes it's something simple like a bowl of chips, but oftentimes it's something fun like a *tortilla, patatas bravas*, or any of the things in this section of the book.

Granada is a city known for its generous tapas, and it's good to know that before you order food with your drink. The first place I went in Granada, we ordered drinks and an order of food. Little did we know that we'd be getting two huge, free tapas in addition!

Legend has it that tapas got their start when King Alfonso XIII ordered a drink in Southern Spain, and to keep sand from blowing into it, the bartender topped it with a piece of *jamón*. The idea stuck and came to be known as a "tapa," which comes from the Spanish word *tapar* ("to put on top of"). Of course, there's debate over how true this is.

Dinner in Spain isn't always the big affair it is in other parts of the world. It's not uncommon to go out around 8:00, order some drinks, eat the tapas that come with, and that's dinner (*"ir de tapas"*)! Light, social, and fun. So have some people over, whip up a few of these tapas, and spend the evening as the Spanish do.

Potatoes with Bravas Sauce

Patatas Bravas

If you've had any Spanish tapas, you've likely had *patatas bravas*. It's everywhere and has become classic. Typically, this dish is made with fried potatoes, but I always go with steamed or roasted potatoes instead. It's a healthier alternative, and let's face it—the real appeal is the sauce, and that's constant across any individual preparation of the potatoes.

Serves 6 - 8

Ingredients

12 red potatoes, washed and quartered
1 teaspoon olive oil
1 teaspoon salt
½ recipe *bravas* sauce (recipe on page 45)

Preheat the oven to 425°F.

Toss the potato quarters with olive oil and salt. Lay on a baking sheet, skin sides against the metal. Bake for 10 – 15 minutes or until browned on the outside and soft on the inside. Move to a serving plate and top with warm *bravas* sauce.

Alternatively, steam the potato quarters until soft but still holding their shape. Move to a serving plate and top with warm *bravas* sauce.

Spanish Omelette
Tortilla de Patatas

For me, the proof that this recipe is a winner is the reaction my friend Ana had when she tried it. Ana is a friend from Madrid who was visiting the U.S., and she came over to make lunch. I told her that I had made a *tortilla de patatas...sin huevo!* (without eggs), and she didn't believe a word I said. When I offered her a piece from the refrigerator, she looked at it skeptically, but when she took a bite, her eyes widened, and she said, "It's very similar! I can't believe it."

So here is my vegan version of a Spanish classic. It is informed tremendously by a variety of Spanish vegan bloggers who turned me onto the notion of using chickpea flour as the base for what becomes a surprisingly eggy omelette. The black salt (Kala Namak) is a tip I picked up from the book **Vegan Brunch** (and is a technique that seems to have caught on amongst vegans looking to eggify the taste of eggless treats) and really does make a difference in this recipe.

Pardon what may seem like a long description. It really is not difficult to make, especially after you've made a couple.

Serves 6

Batter Ingredients

½ cup chickpea/garbanzo bean flour
2 tablespoons nutritional yeast
1 tablespoons tapioca starch
½ teaspoon black salt (Kala Namak)
¾ cup of water
½ cup of nondairy milk

1 tablespoon apple cider vinegar

Omellete Filling

¼ - ½ lb potatoes, peeled & sliced
½ onion, sliced

To prepare the "batter" for the omelette, simply put all of the batter ingredients in a blender and blend until smooth. It may appear to be more liquid than it should be, but have faith! It will firm up quickly in the pan. Leave the batter in the blender for now.

Healthier Version: For the lower-oil version of this recipe, you can steam the potatoes. Start to cook the potatoes first, and you can prepare the rest of the ingredients as they steam (10 minutes or so). When they are done, add the steamed potatoes to the omelette batter. Sauté the onion in 1 teaspoon of olive oil (or water, for an even more low-oil approach). When the onions are done, season to taste and add them to the omelette batter.

Traditional Version: Begin by sautéing the onions in 4-5 tablespoons of olive oil. When the onions are translucent, add the potatoes and cook in the oil until they are tender, 5 – 10 minutes. When the mix is cooked through, remove from the pan with a slotted spoon and add to the omelette batter, leaving as much of the cooking oil in the pan as you can.

When it's time to cook your *tortilla*, lightly mix the potatoes and onions into the batter. Heat 2 tablespoons of olive oil in a small (8" diameter) non-stick pan. You want the oil to be hot before pouring in the omelette mix, so you can test the oil by dropping just a drip of the batter into the oil. If it immediately begins to sizzle sharply, you're ready to go. Otherwise, wait for a bit longer and try again.

When the oil is hot, pour the omelette mix into the pan and reduce the heat to medium. Use the back of spoon to smooth over the top and let the mix cook for a few minutes. The top layer will remain fairly liquid, but you will notice the omelette solidifying and forming something like a crispy outer layer where it comes into contact with the pan.

After 2-3 minutes, it's time to flip the tortilla. It will take a little practice to recognize when it's time to flip, but you're looking for a nice golden color on the underside of the omelette. Unfortunately, you can't see it until you flip it! But generally, you can notice when it seems to easily slip away from the pan.

To do the flipping, get a plate and invert it over the pan. I'm right-handed, so I put my left hand firmly on top of the plate and grip the handle of the pan with my right hand. Over the sink, in one fluid motion, turn over the pan, keeping the plate pressed firmly against it. The *tortilla* should dislodge from the pan and rest on the plate. Remove the pan and just slide the *tortilla* off the plate and back into the pan. The uncooked side of the *tortilla* should now be in direct contact with the pan. Let this cook for another minute or two, using a spatula to lift under the omelette to see how the bottom side is coming along.

There will be some liquid residue on your plate. It happens. You might even have a left over slice of potato that sticks to the plate and doesn't make it back into the pan. No worries. Rinse off the plate so you can use it to serve, and discard any vegetable bits that may have stuck to it.

To serve, take the omelette off the heat, and move it to your plate. You can do this either by sliding right off the pan or doing another pan/plate flipping move. Sometimes it depends on which side looks better. Cut the *tortilla* into 6 or 8 pieces just like you would with a pie. You can serve it warm right then and there, but it's also good cold the next day.

Variations

Don't feel limited to just a potato and onion *tortilla* (*tortilla de patatas con cebolla*). Even though it's the most common version in Spain, people make many different variations.

It's fairly traditional to add zucchini, so you can swap half of the sliced potatoes out for the same volume of sliced zucchini. Cook these with the onion if you opt for the steamed potato method.

Alternatively, I remember seeing a purple tortilla in Barcelona that turned out to be an eggplant omelette. Finally, a friend of mine told me that she makes a *tortilla de peras* on special occasions, replacing the sliced potatoes with sliced pears!

Spanish Meatballs in Sauce

Tapas de Albóndigas

For years, vegans have applied creative ingenuity to cracking the meatless meatball code. It would be bold of me to tout this recipe as the ultimate achievement in vegan meatballs. Instead, my point is to give you a meatball recipe in the context of this classic Spanish tapa. Getting a small plate of meatballs in a sauce, or *albóndigas en salsa*, is a quintessential Spanish delight. Nix the meat, and you've got pretty much the same thing—a small bite of something warm and saucy.

The sauce itself also takes several forms, and I offer three different sauce recipes here. Pick whichever strikes your fancy. It seems that most American renditions of "Spanish Meatballs" use a tomato sauce, which is delicious, but feel free to branch out a bit.

Regardless of the sauce you use, you can serve these either by putting indivudal saucy meatballs on small plates or you can arrange them all on a serving plate with toothpicks in each one.

To start, you'll need to make a batch of "meat"balls. You can make these yourself (see my recipe on page 61) or use store-bought vegan meatballs. Then it's time to finish it up with a sauce.

Sauce #1: Basic Albóndigas Sauce

½ onion, diced
2 cloves of garlic, minced
1 tablespoon all-purpose flour

½ cup white wine
1 cup water or vegetable stock
Pinch of saffron or ½ teaspoon sweet paprika (for color)

If you fried your meatballs in oil, you can just use the same oil to get started. Otherwise, heat a tablespoon of olive oil in a frying pan. When the oil is hot, add the onion and garlic, and cook until just starting to brown.

Add the flour and saffron/paprika. Mix to create a roux. When the flour is incorporated, slowly add the wine, stirring consistently. When it has thickened to a pasty consistency, add the water or stock, stir, and heat to a simmer for 5 minutes or so. Add the cooked meatballs to the sauce and let simmer for 20 minutes. Leave uncovered because you want to sauce to reduce as it cooks.

Sauce #2: Almond Sauce

This is similar to the basic sauce, but it includes fried almonds. For frying, you want almonds without their skins. You can either skin your own almonds by blanching them briefly in boiling water, letting them cool, and sliding their skins off or you can buy blanched, slivered almonds.

    2 tablespoons olive oil
    50g skinned almonds (about 1/3 cup whole almonds)
    2 cloves garlic
    ½ cup panko breadcrumbs
    ½ teaspoon saffron
    ½ teaspoon salt
    ½ cup white wine
    1 cup of water or vegetable broth

Heat the oil in a large frying pan and lightly fry the almonds and garlic cloves until toasted. Remove the almonds and garlic from the oil and add to a blender. In the remaining oil, fry the breadcrumbs until light brown. Add the toasted breadcrumbs, along with the other ingredients, to the blender. Blend everything to a smooth puree.

Pour the blended sauce back to the pan and add the meatballs. Bring to a simmer and keep simmering for another 15 – 20 minutes so the sauce reduces and the meatballs soak up some of the sauce.

Sauce #3: Basic Tomato Sauce

1 teaspoon olive oil
1 small onion, peeled and diced
2 cloves garlic, minced
15 oz can diced tomatoes
1 teaspoon dried basil
1 teaspoon dried oregano
½ teaspoon salt

Heat olive oil in a saucepan and sauté onions until translucent, 4 - 5 minutes. Then add garlic and sauté for another 1 - 2 minutes. Pour all contents of the canned tomatoes to the saucepan, bring to a boil, and let simmer for 10 - 15 minutes.

Stir in basil, oregano and salt. Add the meatballs and let simmer for another 15 minutes or so, allowing the sauce to reduce and the meatballs to soak up some of the sauce.

Garlic Mushrooms
Champiñones al Ajillo

T his simple tapa is great as a snack with drinks or as an appetizer at a party. I made these for a friend visiting from Madrid, and she said it reminded her of her mother's *champiñones*. High praise, indeed!

The key is to get the taste of the garlic in the olive oil, cook the mushrooms well, and add that little punch of lemon at the end. You can eat this on its own with a fork, but it's also common to serve with slices of bread and spoon the mushrooms on the bread (like bruschetta).

Serves 6

Ingredients

3 tablespoons olive oil
2 – 4 cloves garlic, chopped
16 oz white or crimini mushrooms, halved
¼ cup chopped parsley
½ – 1 tablespoon fresh lemon juice
salt

Heat the oil in a large sauté pan and add the garlic. You don't want to brown the garlic much—the main goal is to infuse the oil with the taste of garlic. Once the garlic is aromatic, add the mushrooms. Coat the mushrooms in the oil and let cook on medium heat for 5 – 10 minutes. First the mushrooms will absorb the oil as they cook, and then the mushroom will start to release their liquid. At this point, raise the heat to cook off the liquid, and mix in half the parsley. Once everything is cooked through, mix in the rest of the parsley, give it a good squeeze of lemon juice, and season to taste.

Fried Morcilla Tapa

Tapa de Morcilla Frita

It's so easy to turn vegan *morcilla* into a quick tapa or hors d'oeuvres. Cut your cooled *morcilla* sausages (page 54) into thick slices (about 1 inch thick). Heat some olive oil in a skillet (I like cast iron for this) and fry the *morcilla* slices for about 2 minutes, flip them over and fry another minute or two on the other side. All you want is for the slices to heat through and for there to be a subtle crispiness on the exterior.

Place the lightly fried *morcilla* slices on thin pieces of bread cut from a good baguette, and you've got a quick little tapa.

Spanish Potato Salad

Ensaladilla Rusa

Full disclosure—this isn't much different from potato salad, good ol' potato salad, and for some reason, they call it "Russian Salad." But my friend Pablo is a big fan and gets a small plate of it anytime he sees it.

Ensaladilla rusa is typically made with tuna, but I've replaced it in this recipe with mashed chickpeas, which offer a similar texture and protein boost. Also, don't miss the super Spanish touch: topping the salad with olives. For these olives, don't use the kind you can get in a jar by the pickles at the grocery store. Instead, go for marinated olives with the pits still in there—look to the olive bar at the supermarket for those.

Makes 5 cups

Ingredients

1 lb red potatoes, peeled
1/3 lb carrots, (1 – 2 medium carrots) peeled and diced small
½ cup frozen peas
1 14.5 oz can of chickpeas (or equivalent of cooked chickpeas)
1 tablespoon white wine vinegar (or apple cider vinegar)
½ - 1 teaspoon salt
½ teaspoon ground black pepper
2/3 – 1 cup vegan mayonnaise
Olives, for garnish

Bring a pot of salted water to a boil. Add the peeled whole red potatoes and cook until soft but not falling apart, roughly 15 minutes.

Remove the potatoes and move to a bowl of cold water to halt cooking. While the potatoes cool, add the carrots to the boiling water; cook for 5 minutes or so until soft but with some bite remaining. Once the carrots are done, toss the frozen peas in the water too for just another minute to defrost. Drain the water from the peas and carrots and move the vegetables to a large bowl.

Dice the cooked potatoes into roughly 1-cm cubes and add to the other vegetables in the bowl.

Drain the chickpeas from their canning liquid and mash the beans with a potato masher until no full beans remain, but the texture should still be rough. Add the mashed chickpeas to the vegetables in the bowl.

Add the vinegar, salt, and pepper; mix well. Finally, add the mayonnaise and mix everything well. Cover and refrigerate for a couple hours until cool. To serve, top with olives (allow about 3 per person)

The Royal Botanical Garden in Madrid

Carrots in Vinegar Dressing

Zanahorias Aliñadas

T his refreshing vegetable tapa comes from Cádiz, a city in south-west Spain. It's right on the ocean, situated between Seville and Gibraltar. Its beaches offer welcome relief from the intense heat of a Spanish summer, but so does this simple dish of marinated carrots, served cold.

It seems that the typical way to prepare the dressing is to crush the garlic and whole cumin seeds together with a mortar and pestle, slowly adding the other ingredients in the very same mortar. Since the mortar and pestle seems somewhat less common in the U.S. (and mostly because I don't already have one), you'll be happy to know that this is delicious when prepared without one.

Serve this straight from the fridge for a refreshing tapa or side dish to a larger meal.

Serves 4

Ingredients

4 medium carrots
2 cloves garlic, peeled
½ tablespoon ground cumin
½ tablespoon dried oregano
1 teaspoon smoked paprika (*pimentón dulce*)

¼ cup apple cider vinegar
¼ cup good olive oil
½ teaspoon salt

Peel the carrots and cut them into ½-inch thick circles. Skinnier carrots work better for this, but if all you have access to are those monstrously wide carrots that pop up occasionally, begin by cutting them lengthwise so you end up with half moons instead of circles.

Bring a small pot of salted water to a boil and add the carrots. Reduce heat to a simmer and let cook until you end up with softer, cooked carrots that still have some bite to them (about 5 – 10 minutes).

While the carrots are cooking, crush the garlic cloves with the side of your knife and finely mince them. You want the mince to be quite fine but not so fine that all the texture is lost. In a small bowl, mix together the minced garlic and the rest of the ingredients, plus ¼ cup of water in which the carrots are cooking.

When the carrots are done, drain off the water and add the cooked carrots to the dressing. Mix the dressing and the carrots well, cover, and refrigerate for a couple hours until cool. Once it has cooled and the carrots have marinated in the vinegary dressing, scoop out the carrots into a serving bowl or straight onto a plate with a slotted spoon. Spoon some of the excess dressing over the carrots as you'd like.

Fried Eggplant with Molasses

Berenjenas Fritas con Miel de Caña

This was one of the first things I ate when I arrived in Granada. It's simple, but it's a classic Granada tapa. What makes the original so special is the particular sweet syrup that's drizzled on top—*miel de caña*. It's unique to this part of the world and hard to find in the U.S. Instead, a drizzle of molasses or agave nectar will do just fine in its place.

Serves 4

Ingredients

1 medium eggplant
1 teaspoon salt
12 oz bottle of seltzer water
¼ cup all purpose flour
¼ cup molasses or agave nectar
1 - 2 cups canola oil, for frying

Slice eggplant into 1-inch circles and cut into half moons. Salt eggplant pieces and let rest for ½ hour in a colander so it releases its liquid.

Soak the salted and drained eggplant in seltzer water for a half hour. Afterward, pat dry and then shake in a large plastic bag with flour to coat.

Pan fry the coated eggplant pieces (only a few at a time), sprinkle with a pinch of salt, and drizzle molasses or agave nectar on top.

Stuffed Tomatoes

Tomates Rellenos

These little stuffed tomatoes are weirdly addictive. The recipe is simple, but filling the cherry tomatoes can be a little tricky. You'll get the hang of it, and even if they look a little messy your first time around, just trust that they'll taste good anyway.

Each bite is a delightful blend of bright acidity from the tomato, saltiness from the olives, and creaminess from the mayo. You'll have trouble stopping yourself!

These are also often made with larger tomatoes, and while they would be easier to stuff, I'm a little put off by the huge amount of mayo that would go in each one. So for me, although they are trickier to put together, the cherry tomato route is the better option.

Makes 30 tiny servings

Ingredients

¼ cup pitted green olives; finely chopped
2 cloves garlic, finely minced
1 tablespoon chopped parsley
¼ cup vegan mayonnaise
30 cherry tomatoes

First, simply mix the chopped olives, garlic, and parsley into the mayo. This will be your filling.

With a paring knife, cut a hole around the stem end of each cherry tomato. The goal is to create a well that runs through the middle of the tomato to make room for the stuffing but to leave as much of the tomato flesh as possible intact. When you've made the well, you can gently squeeze out some of the seeds and inner juice to make more room for the stuffing.

To stuff, I create a makeshift piping bag out of regular plastic sandwich bag. Put the filling into a plastic bag and cut away a small bit of one of the bag's non-zipper corners. This hole in the corner should be big enough to let the olive chunks through but small enough that you can get the tip into the cherry tomato wells. Now start squeezing away!

Fill each tomato with the filling. Although it can look a little more attractive if you can get some of the stuffing to pile up over the top of the hole, I find that it's more trouble than it's worth. You can just fill the cherry tomato wells to the top.

You can serve these right away at room temperature, but they're also good after a brief (roughly 1 hour) chill in the refrigerator.

Segovia

Canary Island Wrinkly Potatoes

Papas Arrugadas

I first learned the term *"arrugadas"* because of a Spanish cartoon of the same name. The movie is about a group of elderly people living in a retirement home. *Arrugadas*, it turns out, means "wrinkles."

This unique dish from the Canary Islands features an interesting and delicious way to prepare tiny potatoes, which develops a wrinkly exterior while maintaining a hot, creamy interior. Serve these topped with one or both of the *mojo* sauces described elsewhere in this book.

Serves 6

Ingredients

1 ½ lbs small potatoes (baby new potatoes or fingerling potatoes)
2 – 3 tablespoons salt
½ cup *mojo picon* (page 51) and/or *mojo verde* (page 52)

Wash the potatoes, put them in a pot with the salt, and add enough water just to cover them. Boil, uncovered, for 20 minutes or so, until the potatoes are tender. Remove the water and put the potatoes back into the empy pot. Keep the dry potatoes over the heat for another 2 – 3 minutes until they dry up, their skins wrinkle, and a salty exterior develops.

Serve hot, topped with *mojo picon* and/or *mojo verde*.

Eggplant Rolls

Rollitos de Berenjena

I made these for a party once, and they were a big hit. As I've looked over the countless vegetable-based tapas, I was always struck by how these *rollitos* looked. Simple and alluring, this tapa uses thinly sliced and roasted eggplant like lasagna noodles, wrapped around a creamy stuffing.

There are tons of ways to stuff a *rollito de berenjena*, many of which include meat. For this recipe, though, I went with a creamy cashew ricotta. You can add a number of tasty vegetabls to this. Here, I use shiitake mushrooms, but let your imagination run wild.

Makes about 10 small rolls

Ingredients

2 medium eggplants
½ lb shiitake mushrooms, chopped
3 tablespoons olive oil

Cashew Ricotta

1 ½ cups cashews, soaked for at least 4 hours
2 tablespoons olive oil
1 tablespoon apple cider vinegar, white wine vinegar, or lemon juice
1 teaspoon salt
¼ teaspoon ground black pepper
1 tablespoon sauerkraut (optional)
½ cup chopped parsley

Pre-heat the oven to 375 °F.

Cut off the tops of the eggplants and slice lengthwise into ¼-inch slices. The result is a bunch of eggplant slices about the same size as lasagna noodles.

Spray a baking sheet with oil and arrange the eggplant slices on the pan. Spray the tops of the slices with a little more oil, and bake for 10 minutes. Flip the slices over and bake for another 10 minutes. The result should be eggplant slices that are easily folded and rolled. Let cool for a few minutes before handling

While the eggplant slices are in the oven, sauté the mushrooms in the remaining olive oil until fully cooked and flavorful. Let cool.

To make the cashew cheese, simply add all of the ingredients except the parsley to a food processor. Process until you achieve a smooth, creamy puree. Add the parsley and pulse a few times to incorporate.

Time to prepare the *rollitos*. Take a slice of eggplant and spoon about 1 tablespoon of the cashew cheese mix onto one end. Scoop about a tablespoon of mushrooms on top of the cashew cheese and roll the eggplant slice around the filling.

Lower the oven's temperature to 350 °F. Place each roll into a baking dish, seam-side down, and bake uncovered for 15 minutes to re-heat all of the components.

Consider serving topped with the tomato sauce recipe presented in the section on *albóndigas* (page 70).

Note

As another tasty variation, you can substitute the mushrooms for slices of roasted red peppers.

Roasted Pepper Salad

Escalivada

This popular Catalan dish celebrates the unparalleled flavor of grilled vegetables. In fact, its name comes from the Catalan word, *"escalivar,"* which is "to cook in ashes." Traditionally, this dish is prepared by roasting peppers straight in coals.

Although you can serve it at any temperature, I prefer it cold/room temperature. Get some good wine and crusty bread, and top bread slices with spoonfuls of this *escalivada,* and you've got a seriously tasty tapa that personifies the simplicity of a laid back summer day in Spain. This also makes a great topping to a grilled veggie burger.

Makes 2 cups

Ingredients

1 red bell pepper
1 orange bell pepper
1 yellow bell pepper
1 tomato
1 tablespoon olive oil
2 shallots, peeled and chopped
1 clove garlic, chopped
¼ cup chopped parsley

Set the broiler to high. Cut each bell pepper in half and remove the stems and seeds. Lay each half (inside down—the skin should be exposed to the fire) on a foil-lined baking sheet. Put under the broiler for about 10 minutes.

Cut the tomato in half. After the peppers have been in the broiler for 10 minutes, add the tomato to the baking sheet, also cut-side down. Keep everything under the broiler for another 10 – 15 minutes.

At this point, the skins of the vegetables should be blackened and blistering. Turn off the broiler, and move the pepper and tomato halves to a bowl and cover with a kitchen towel to let cool.

When cool enough to handle, pull the peels off the peppers and tomato. They should come right off, but it can be helpful to do this under running water at the kitchen sink. Discard the peels and chop the roasted peppers and tomato into slices.

Heat the olive oil in a sauté pan and sauté the shallot and garlic for 2 – 3 minutes. Add the roasted vegetable slices to the hot pan and toss with the shallot mix for 2 – 3 minutes. Mix in parsley and season with salt.

Serve warm or cold.

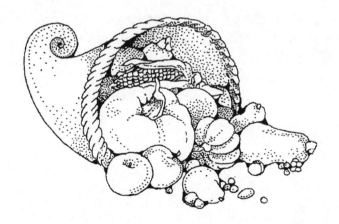

Morning Toast with Tomato

Pan con Tomate

This isn't anything revolutionary, but it's my breakfast of choice in Spain. It's so simple and unpretentious, but it's perfectly satisfying in the morning alongside a *café solo* (espresso) or cup of good coffee. The idea is basically tomato guts on toast with some salt and olive oil. That's it. And it's perfect.

There are a few ways to do this. The super Spanish way is to just squeeze and scrape half a tomato on a piece of toast until the bread is coated with the tomato's insides. Another method is one I noticed in a little café one morning in Lavapies, Madrid, and it's my go-to method...mostly because I never developed the knack for the scraping method.

This method just involves processing a few tomatoes at once, and it lets you serve out breakfast for several people at the same time. It also lets you keep a jar of the simplest tomato sauce in the world in the refrigerator to prepare a few days' worth of breakfast at once. It's not much of a recipe, but I've translated the process to recipe speak:

Ingredients

A piece of a good baguette, about 5 inches long
1 tablespoon good Spanish olive oil
Pinch of salt
2 - 3 tomatoes

To make the tomato "sauce," peel the tomatoes by submerging them in boiling water for 30 seconds and then moving them to an ice bath—the peels will just slide right off. Drop the peeled tomatoes in a blender or food processor and pulse a few times. You're not trying to make tomato puree, just breaking up the tomato into something scoopable. Keep whatever you don't use in a jar in the refrigerator for tomorrow's breakfast, but remember that this is still raw tomato, and it won't be good forever.

To assembe: Cut your baguette in half lengthwise, like you're making a sandwich. Toast the bread in a toaster, or if you don't have a toaster, you can heat some olive oil in a pan and toast the non-crust side of the baguette pieces in the pan (like you're making a grilled cheese).

Scoop some of the tomato with a spoon and spread it over the toasted baguette pieces. Drizzle the top with olive oil and sprinkle with salt to your liking.

The Menu del Día

There's a great concept around lunchtime in Spain: the *menu del día*. It is essentially a fixed-price lunch menu with several options for a full multi-course meal at an affordable price. Taking this route for lunch means you get a first course (*primero*), a second course (*segundo*), and a dessert course (*postre*). You can also usually choose to have a coffee instead of dessert. To top it all off, these lunch menus include a bread and a drink (wine, beer, water, whatever)!

Unfortunately, options available for the second are nearly always meat dishes. So I've gotten used to politely asking if I could take two first course options for my meal. If there was ever a confused look, a friend of mine would pipe in and say, "*Él es vegetariano*" and they'd all have a good chuckle over it.

Common first course options include many of the things covered elsewhere in this book, including *gazpacho* (page 18), *samorejo* (page 27), *tortilla Española* (page 65), as well as good ol' fashioned side salad. Desserts often featured *natillas*, *flan*, *arroz con leche*, as well as fruits and yogurts.

For Dinner

When in Spain, I spent so much time enjoying tapas and menus de dia that I didn't have too many full meals in the way we traditionally think of them. At least one reason for this is that Spanish entrees are pretty heavy on the meat.

There were a few stand-out experiences, though, that qualified as full meals. These include huge pans of *paella*, an afternoon of *cocido madrileño*, and my all-time favorite, *pisto*.

I've also learned about delicious Spanish vegetable dishes that make for perfect sides to a vegan dinner. Smoked paprika-infused mashed potatoes, pine nut-riddled Swiss chard, and simple vegetable purees. These are sides that wouldn't necessarily work as well as tapas, but rest assured, virtually any tapa would be great as a side dish for dinner.

Simple Vegetable Paella

Paella de Sartén

I would be crazy not to include a *paella* recipe in a book about Spanish cooking. If people can think of only one example of Spanish cuisine (assuming they don't think *burritos* are Spanish), they're likely to think *paella*. There's something wonderful about the spirit of *paella*—it's cooked in massive pans (called *paelleras*), and it's meant to be shared by a big group of people. In fact, it's common for a group to eat straight out of the *paellera*.

We're not always cooking for the masses, though, and if you don't already own a *paellera*, you may not want to spend the money just to try your hand at making this classic Spanish rice dish. Luckily, you can pull off a pretty legitimate *paella* in a stainless steel skillet right on your stovetop.

There's one element that you lose with the stovetop version, though. Many say that the best part of *paella* is the *"socarrat,"* which is the crispy layer of rice where it meets the bottom of the pan. Traditional *paelleras* are made thin enough to apply an even, direct heat that crisps up that bottom layer. Getting that in a skillet is less likely, but the resulting rice is just as tasty.

Serves 3-4

Ingredients

1 tablespoon olive oil
½ small onion, peeled, and diced
2 cloves garlic, minced
½ small green bell pepper, seeded and diced
4 oz chopped mushrooms
1 tomato, diced (or 1 cup canned diced tomatoes)
½ teaspoon of salt (depending on saltiness of broth)
1 cup Arborio rice (or *Bomba* rice, if you can find it)
2 cups vegetable broth
½ teaspoon saffron, crushed
Lemon wedges, for serving

Start by bringing the vegetable broth to a low simmer in a saucepan, and add the saffron. You want the broth to be warm when you add it to the rice in a little bit.

With the broth still slowly simmering, heat the olive oil in a large skillet and add the chopped onion and green pepper. Sauté for 4 – 5 minutes and add the garlic, cooking for another 2 – 3 minutes. Add the mushroom and continue to cook another 3 – 4 minutes. Finally add the tomatoes and cook over medium heat until most of the liquid has evaporated.

At this point I like to season the vegetables with salt because you won't get another chance to season the *paella*. Keep in mind, though, how salty the broth is—you don't want to end up with rice that's too salty.

Mix the rice into the cooked vegetable mix, and make sure everything is spread into an even layer in the skillet. Add the vegetable saffron-infused broth to the skillet, bring to a boil, and reduce heat and simmer for about 15 minutes. At first, the broth should cover the rice by about an inch, but of course, as it cooks the water level will reduce as it's absorbed by the rice.

It's very important that you don't mix the *paella* anymore. Everything should remain untouched in the pan until you're ready to serve.

When most of the water seems to have been absorbed (15 minutes, of course, is a guide, so you want to keep an eye on it so it doesn't burn), remove from the heat and let it rest for about 5 minutes while the rice soaks up any remaining liquid.

Serve with lemon wedges—a quick squirt of the lemon juice really brightens everything up.

Variations

This is just a base recipe. Feel free to doctor it up with any other vegetables you'd like. I like to make it with shredded carrot and peas, but other vegetables like artichokes, red pepper, and green beans are typical as well.

If you want to try making a *paella* in a real *paellera*, the instructions are exactly the same, but of course, you'll need to adjust the quantities accordingly!

Saffron

Azafrán

G rowing up, somehow I had learned that saffron is the world's most expensive spice. It's for this reason that I probably avoided the idea altogether when I started to enjoy cooking. However, despite its shocking sticker price, you only need a little bit at a time, making it a viable ingredient in many Spanish kitchens.

Saffron threads are actually the stamens of a particular type of flower—the crocus. These purple flowers bloom for only about a week during the whole year, and in that time, the saffron threads must be picked swiftly or the opportunity is lost until next year. Not only that, but the threads must be picked by hand and then carefully dried, making the whole process very labor-intensive and the product a rarity. In fact, just one gram of saffron can depend on as many as 200 crocus flowers. This, of course, sheds light on why this spice commands such a high price.

So it must be good, right? It would be a shame to spend all that time collecting flower stamens that have no beneficial effect on food. Saffron has had an enduring influence on Spanish cuisine. Perhaps most notably, saffron plays an important role in making *paella*. Because of its price, people will sometimes substitute a product known as *colorante*, which includes things like turmeric to impart the bright saffron yellow color to a *paella*. But for the most authentic experience, nothing beats true Spanish saffron for its taste and color.

Because saffron can be so pricey, you may be tempted to cut some corners. For this product, though, price is a good indicator of quality. Lower priced saffron products may not even be saffron but instead, a plant akin to bark that's been colored and washed with chemical additives. In other words, it's not what you want.

Ground saffron is also something to stay away from. Even if it started as real saffron, the ground version will lose its pungency quickly. It's also less likely to be real saffron in the first place. "Ground saffron" often includes some combination of fake saffron product, paprika, and turmeric.

I hadn't ever cooked with saffron before I embarked on my Spanish cooking adventure, and I have to say that it's a fun little spice to deal with. Such a small amount imparts such a unique and authentic flavor to rice dishes. Look for saffron at any spice market that deals at a high quality, and you won't be disappointed.

Madrid-Style Winter Stew

Cocido Madrileño

Although I don't care for the meaty part of *cocido*, I love the **idea** behind *cocido*. It's a full meal fit for a big group. It brings people together and warms everyone when it's cold out.

Traditionally, *cocido* consists of beans, vegetables, meat, and noodles, and everything is cooked together over low heat for a long time. All of the flavors co-mingle, and the result is a veritable feast. Because it takes so long to cook, it's a great excuse to bring people together around 11:00, open up some wine, and hang out while the aroma begins to fill the air and the simmering pot heats the whole kitchen. By about 2:00, it's time to dig right in for a long, relaxed lunch.

Vegan *cocido* doesn't take quite as long and does away with what Spaniards would likely call the focus (i.e., the meat). A traditional *cocido* includes an array of meats—chicken, pork, *chorizo*, *morcilla*—you name it. The result is a complex broth that some would say is the real appeal of *cocido*, referred to only by the Spanish word for "broth," *caldo*. In fact, during the winter in Spain, it's not uncommon for bars to offer a shot of hot *caldo* as a quick and tasty warm-up.

Rest assured, though...vegan *cocido madrileño* is possible, and it's a thing of beauty. With meat out of the picture, the focus turns to a delicious *pimentón*-infused vegetable broth, slow-cooked garbanzo beans, and simple winter vegetables. You can even include veggie meats to approximate the "real thing," but it's no requirement.

Serves 4 - 6

Ingredients

8 cups good quality vegetable broth
2 tablespoons olive oil
1 tablespoon smoked paprika (*pimentón dulce*)
1 lb dry garbanzo beans (chickpeas)
3 russet potatoes, peeled
6 – 8 carrots, peeled
1 head of cabbage, chopped into ribbons
8 oz vermicelli or angel hair noodles
1 teaspoon salt (+ 2 teaspoons for brining the beans)

For best results, brine the dry garbanzo beans overnight. To do so, put them in a bowl and fill with water, covering the beans by about 2 inches. Mix in 2 teaspoons of salt and let soak overnight.

On cooking day, your goal is to get the beans, potatoes, carrots, and cabbage to doneness at the same time. Cooking times vary, so I'm giving you this goal upfront so you can have it in mind as you go forward.

When ready to start cooking, drain the garbanzos from their soaking liquid and put them in a large stock pot. Add in the oil and paprika, pour the vegetable broth over the beans, and bring everything to a boil. Reduce heat to low and let simmer for an hour and a half, or until the chickpeas taste just about done.

At this point, add in the peeled potatoes and carrots—go ahead and put them in whole—and let cook for 20 minutes longer.

While the vegetables cook with the beans, scoop out about 2 cups of the broth and transfer to an extra saucepan. Bring to a boil and add the cabbage, cooking it for 15 – 20 minutes. Salt to taste.

You want to reach a point where the garbanzo beans are cooked through—soft but not mushy—and the potatoes and carrots are similarly cooked. You want to be able to easily cut through them with a knife without them losing their shape.

With tongs, remove the potatoes and carrots and let rest on a plate. With a slotted spoon or a small strainer, remove the cooked garbanzos and move to a serving bowl. Drain the cabbage, letting the broth filter back into the main pot; move the cabbage to its own serving dish.

Bring the broth back to a boil. Break the bunch of vermicelli noodles into four smaller pieces, and add these to the broth, letting them cook to proper pasta doneness. Serve this simple noodle soup as a starter and then bring out the other plates to serve the slow cooked simple vegetables and beans family style (with some good bread, of course).

Note

If you want to incorporate the vegan *chorizo* (page 56) and/or *morcilla* (page 54), I suggest cutting the sausages into round pieces, frying on each side in a bit of olive oil, and giving them a quick soak in the broth to pick up the flavors. This can all be done in the last few minutes of cooking (while the noodle soup is simmering). You can then serve these Spanish "meats" on their own plate.

Summer Stewed Vegetables

Pisto

When summer hits, I become a *pisto* machine. When the farmers market overflows with eggplant, zuccini, and tomatoes, I can't help myself. This is a dish that celebrates the simple flavors of these perfect vegetables. It's very similar to *ratatouille*.

As with everything, there are plenty of ways to make *pisto*. Sometimes it's really chunky, and sometimes it's blended smooth. Also, typical of *pisto manchego*, a fried egg usually tops a hot bowl of the vegetable stew. If you eat eggs, you can consider doing this, but I find it every bit as satisfying on its own.

This recipe comes from my Spanish friend Bea, who got it from her mother, so you can trust its authenticity. Although, speaking of authenticity, I usually serve *pisto* on top of couscous or pasta, but don't tell Bea I said that.

Serves 4

Ingredients

1 – 2 tablespoons olive oil
1 medium onion, diced
2 cloves of garlic, minced
1 green bell pepper, diced (about 1 cup)
1 red bell pepper, diced (about 1 cup)

2 zucchini, diced (about 3 cups)
1 eggplant, peeled and diced (about 3 cups)
4 medium tomatoes, peeled, seeded, and diced (or a 28 oz can diced tomatoes)
1 teaspoon salt

Heat the oil in a heavy-bottomed pot. Add the onion and garlic and cook until translucent and aromatic. Go through the ingredients list in order, adding the next ingredient and cooking for about 5 minutes, then adding the next ingredient and cooking for about 5 minutes, etc. Each time, the flavor of one vegetable will integrate with the ones that came before it. After you add the tomatoes, stir to mix everything, put the lid on the pot, and let simmer over low to medium heat for 30 – 40 minutes.

Taste and season with salt. If there is still a lot of liquid in the pot (it should not be soupy), let simmer with the lid off for another 10 minutes or so to let the liquid evaporate.

Serve on its own as a side or to make it a more substantial main dish, serve over couscous or pasta.

Rice and Veggie-Stuffed Eggplant

Berenjenas Rellenas

S tuffing eggplants is a popular tradition in Spain, but a lot of people stuff them with meat and/or cheese. This recipe maintains the spirit of a Spanish stuffed eggplant but does so without the animal products. The presentation is a fun way to eat grains and vegetables. I've made these with brown rice, white rice, couscous, and quinoa, but of course, you can choose whatever seems best to you.

Serves 4

Ingredients

2 medium eggplants
1 red bell pepper, seeded and diced fine
1 onion, diced fine
2 cloves garlic, minced
28 oz can diced tomatoes
2 cups prepared rice, quinoa, or couscous
1 teaspoon salt
1/3 cup breadcrumbs (optional)

Pre-heat the oven to 350°F

Cut each eggplant in half lengthwise. With a paring knife, cut a cross-hatch pattern into the flesh of the eggplant (see the illustration), just barely reaching the skin of the eggplant on the other side. This will help steam the eggplant more quickly and make scooping easier. Put each half of the eggplant on a plate, cover with plastic wrap, and microwave for 3 minutes. The eggplant halves should retain their shape, but the inner flesh should be soft. Let these rest until cool enough to handle. If you're making the full recipe, you'll probably only have room in your microwave to handle two halves at a time.

While the eggplant is steaming and cooling, heat 3 tablespoons of water in a sauté pan and add the onions, garlic, and red pepper (if you want to go a more traditional route, you can sauté in 1 tablespoon of olive oil). When the vegetables are translucent, mix in the smoked paprika, and pour in the canned tomatoes. Continue to cook everything until most of the liquid has evaporated and you have a thick, tomato-y sauce.

In a large bowl, combine the rice, quinoa, or couscous, the tomato sauce, and salt. Scoop out the inner flesh of the eggplant halves, coarsely chop, and add to the bowl, leaving behind hollow eggplant "bowls." Note that you don't want to scrape all of the eggplant flesh away—a thin lining along the skin will help the eggplant bowls keep their shape. Give the stuffing a good mix.

Move the eggplant bowls onto a baking sheet and stuff each one with the rice and vegetable stuffing. If using, top each stuffed eggplant half with a thin layer of breadcrumbs and bake in the oven for 20 minutes.

Serve warm.

SCORING THE EGGPLANT FLESH

Butter

Mantequilla

You may have noticed that the vegan favorite, Earth Balance, is missing from this book. One thing that makes it easier to translate Spanish cooking to a vegan diet is that the cooking fat of choice is almost always olive oil, which is already vegan.

When I mentioned to my Spanish friends that I would be traveling to Paris one weekend, they scoffed and said, "they use so much butter—everything is so heavy." It struck me as funny that these friends of mine, who happily eat foods containing cured pork, cheese, and olive oil were so averse to the fattiness of butter.

Spanish Mashed Potatoes

Patatas Revolconas

T his is essentially the Spanish version of mashed potatoes. It does away with the elements that you may think define mashed potatoes—butter and cream—and replaces them with distinctly Spanish flavors—olive oil and *pimentón* (smoked paprika). These red-tinted mashed potatoes can be served as a first course, a side dish, and can even be the star of a meatless meal.

As with a lot of Spanish food, this is a dish that typically highlights meat flavors. *Patatas revolconas* are classically served with bacon or slices of *chorizo*. The idea is to first cook the meat in oil, remove the meat, and use the remaining fat to briefly bring out the flavor of the paprika and incorporate into the potatoes. This recipe does away with the meat (but see the notes) and focuses on the potatoes, the oil, and the *pimentón*.

Serves 4

Ingredients

1 ½ lbs of potatoes, peeled (about 8 red potatoes or 4 russet potatoes)
¾ cup of the potatoes' cooking liquid
¼ cup of olive oil
1 tablespoon smoked paprika (*pimentón dulce*)
1 teaspoon ground cayenne pepper (optional)
½ - 1 teaspoon salt

Peel the potatoes and chop them into big chunks. Bring a pot of salted water (enough to cover the potatoes) to a boil and add the potatoes. Let cook until they can be easily pierced with a fork.

When the potatoes are done, reserve ¾ cup of the cooking water, drain the potatoes, and add the reserved water back to the pot along with the potatoes. Mash up the potatoes with a fork or a potato masher.

Heat the olive oil in a separate small pan, and when the oil is hot, add the smoked paprika and ground hot red pepper (if using) and let the spice bloom in the oil for 10 seconds until fragrant. Add the hot oil and spice to the mashed potatoes and whisk everything together until the potatoes are smooth and the spice is incorporated throughout. Finish it off by adding salt to taste (about 1 teaspoon).

Notes

To bring a bit of the original Spanish flare back into this, consider chopping up some tempeh bacon or slicing up a vegan Spanish *chorizo* sausage and cooking it in the oil first. When the vegan bacon/*chorizo* is cooked, take it out of the oil and reserve on a plate for later. Use the oil to bloom the smoked paprika and go from there. When you serve the *patatas revolconas*, add some bits of the bacon/*chorizo* to the top as a garnish.

Chard with Raisins & Pine Nuts

Acelgas con Pasas y Piñones

I don't have much to say about this other than that it's delicious. Cooked greens with a slight sweetness from the raisins and a light texture from the pine nuts? It's a perfect vegetable side. Pine nuts are quite common in Spanish food, but they are expensive in the U.S. For this, though, the extra cost is worth it for the soft, buttery crunch they add to this dish.

Serves 4 - 6

Ingredients

¼ cup golden raisins
¼ cup pine nuts
2 tablespoons olive oil
1 shallot, chopped
2 pounds Swiss Chard
Salt, to taste

First, plump the raisins with a cup of hot or boiling water for 20 minutes or so.

While the raisins are rehydrating, dry toast the pine nuts in a skillet for 3 – 5 minutes. Keep them moving so that they don't burn. Aim for a nice golden coating. Once golden and fragrant, move to a plate to cool.

Prepare the chard by first removing the tough stems and chop into small pieces. Then coarsely chop the leaves.

Heat the olive oil in a pan and sauté the shallot for a few minutes until fragrant and translucent. Add the chopped chard stems and sauté for 2 – 3 minutes. Finally, add the chopped chard leaves, allowing them to wilt for 3 – 5 minutes and remove from heat. You don't want to fully cook the greens down—instead you're aiming just to wilt them.

Drain the raisins from their soaking liquid, and add them and the toasted pine nuts to the chard. Toss all of the ingredients together, season with salt, and serve warm.

Notes

You can also consider using spinach or beet greens in place of the chard.

Toledo

Creamy Vegetable Puree

Puré de Verduras

A kin to creamy mashed potatoes, Spanish *pures* can include all sorts of vegetables and not just potatoes.

Serves 4 - 6

Ingredients

4 carrots, peeled and chopped
1 zucchini, stemmed and chopped
1 leek, chopped (white part only)
2 potatoes, peeled and chopped
1 teaspoon salt
3 cups water
Chives, for garnsih

Put the chopped vegetable pieces in a soup pot, add water and salt, and bring to a boil. Reduce to a simmer for 20 minutes or until all vegetable pieces are soft. Move to a blender (or use a hand blender) and blend until very smooth. The consistency should approximate thin mashed potatoes.

Serve with a sprinkling of chopped chives for garnish.

Puente de Arganzuela en el Parque Madrid Río

Thanks!

I t's been so much fun to put this cookbook together. It's been a crazy couple of years, trying so many recipes, some successful and some not so successful (Spanish *croquetas* continue to elude me).

Through these recipes, I hope you've gained an appreciation for the simple deliciousness of Spanish cooking. Whether you're throwing a tapas party, inviting people over for *cocido*, or just having a nice dinner with wine and *pisto*, may your Spanish adventure be a fun one!

Spanish/English Glossary

You may find it handy to consult a simple glossary of food and cooking terms. This is by no means complete, but it should cover you for most things. Also, with a few exceptions, terms referring to meat, eggs, and dairy have been omitted.

A

aceite: oil
aceituna: olive
agua: water
ajo: garlic
albahaca: basil
albóndiga: meatball
alcachofa: artichoke
aliño: dressing
alioli: garlic mayonnaise
almendra: almond
anacardo: cashew
apio: celery
arroz: rice
asado: roasted
azafrán: saffron
azúcar: sugar

B

batata: sweet potato
berenjena: eggplant
bocadillo: sandwich

C

calabacín: zucchini
calabaza: pumpkin
caldo: broth
cayena: cayenne
cazuela: casserole
cebolla: onion
cebolleta: green onion, scallion
cebollino: chive
cereza: cherry
cerveza: beer
champiñon: mushroom
chorizo: red spiced sausage
cocina: kitchen
coliflor: cauliflower
comida: food, lunch

crema: cream

D

desayuno: breakfast
diente de ajo: clove of garlic
dulce: sweet

E

ensalada: salad
entremeses: hors-d'ouevre
escabeche: marinade
espárrago: asparagus
especia: spice
espinaca: spinach

F

faba: type of bean
fideo: vermicelli

fresa: strawberry
frito: fried
fruta: fruit

G

galleta: cookie
garbanzo: chickpea
guisante: pea

H

harina: flour
helado: ice cream
hierbabuena: mint
horno: oven
huevo: egg

J

jamón: ham
Jerez: sherry wine
judía: green bean

L

leche: milk
lechuga: lettuce
lenteja: lentil
lima: lime
limón: lemon

M

maíz: corn
mantequilla: butter
manzana: apple
mayonesa: mayonnaise
melaza: molasses

melocotón: peach
melón: melon
menta: mint
miel: honey
morcilla: blood sausage
mostaza: mustard

N

naranja: orange
nata: cream
nuez: nut

O

olla: pot

P

pan: bread
parrilla: grill
pastel: pastry
patata: potato
pepino: cucumber
pera: pear
perejil: parsley
picante: hot, spicy
pimentón: paprika
pimienta: pepper (spice)
pimiento: pepper (vegetable)
piña: pineapple
piñón: pine nut
plancha: grill
puerro: leek

Q

queso: cheese

R

repollo: cabbage

S

sal: salt
salado: salted, salty
salsa: sauce
saltear: to saute
sandía: watermelon
sarten: frying pan
seta: wild mushroom
sidra: cider
soya: soy
sopa: soup

T

tomate: tomato
tortilla: omelet
tostado: toasted
trigo: wheat

U

uva: grape

V

verdura: vegetable
vino: wine

Z

zanahoria: carrot

Index

A

B

C